Original title:
Art and Soul

Editor: Theodor Taimla
Author: Rachelle Randvee
ISBN HARDBACK: 978-9916-759-90-5
ISBN PAPERBACK: 978-9916-759-91-2

Chiseled Thoughts

In marble halls of silent grace,
Ideas carve their timeless place.
Each chisel strike, a fleeting blink,
An echo, as the thinkers think.

The sculptor's hand, so deft and bold,
Shapes dreams within the stone, so cold.
From rough to smooth, the visions rise,
A testament to seeking skies.

Chips of clarity fall away,
To show the light of break of day.
With every line and curve refined,
The masterpiece within aligned.

Mind and matter intertwine,
In silent dance, the purest sign,
That thought, once raw, with art becalmed,
Finds form, in chisel breathing calm.

In this gallery of inner sight,
Where shadows play with beams of light,
Chiseled thoughts forever stand,
Crafted by the artist's hand.

Resonant Forms

Upon the strings of silken air,
Echoes drift, beyond compare.
Resonance in forms unseen,
Whispers on the twilight scene.

A melody in twilight's reach,
Hums a story, soft to breach.
Each note a tale, in fragments born,
Resonance till breaking dawn.

In the silence, shadows stir,
Between the notes, they intersperse.
Harmonics in the still declare,
Formed in spaces, pure and rare.

Cadence flows like rivers deep,
Through the soul, where secrets keep.
Resonating truths unfold,
In harmonies both brave and bold.

The world in form, in resonant ties,
Across the skies, the music flies.
Shapes of sound, in waves transform,
A symphony in resonant forms.

Fleeting Brushstrokes

On canvas bare, where dreams reside,
In hues of dawn, emotions glide.
A whisper soft, a shadow bright,
A fleeting image caught in light.

Each stroke a tale, each hue a song,
In moments brief, our hearts belong.
The art of time, elusive mark,
In transient splendor, life embarks.

Colors blend, they dance, they fade,
Yet memories in pigments laid.
A portrait's gaze, a fleeting sigh,
Ephemeral brushstrokes passing by.

Chromatic Epiphanies

In colors' arms, our spirits soar,
Where silent truths are found once more.
A palette rich, with no disguise,
Reveals the secrets in our eyes.

Each shade, a whisper of the soul,
Together forming something whole.
A symphony of light and shade,
Where countless epiphanies are made.

Through vibrant bursts and muted tones,
A world unseen, a heart foretold.
In chromatic dreams we find,
The epiphanies that free the mind.

Symphony of Shades

Beneath the sun, beneath the moon,
A symphony of shades in tune.
Dark meets light in perfect rhymes,
Eternal dance through endless times.

The shadows waltz, the colors sway,
In twilight's gentlest embrace.
A harmony in dusk and dawn,
Where all of nature sings along.

With every hue, with every tone,
A melody in silence grown.
The symphony of shades unfurls,
A painted song that fills our world.

Ephemeral Murals

On ancient walls, the stories spin,
In murals old and layers thin.
A fleeting glimpse of days gone by,
An echo of a whispered sigh.

Patterns fade, yet still they speak,
Of lives once lived, of souls unique.
In crumbling art, the past resides,
An everlasting, transient guide.

Murals tell of joy and pain,
In sunlit rays or tear-filled rain.
Each stroke a moment, brief and pure,
In ephemeral beauty, memories endure.

Emotive Palette

Colors swirl on canvas pure,
A dance of joy and sorrow's lure,
Crimson dreams in twilight's call,
Pastel whispers as nightfall.

Each hue tells tales of heart's embrace,
Brushstrokes paint love's tender face,
Emerald hopes in morning's gleam,
Azure thoughts in silent dream.

Motions delicate, strokes so light,
Shadows play in soft moonlight,
Golden traces of laughter's cheer,
Midnight blues of hidden fear.

From palette's edge to soul's deep core,
Emotions thrive, forevermore,
In every shade, a story fused,
By every layer, hearts mused.

Splashes of Essence

Droplets of color on life's page,
Echoes of joy, whispers of age,
Lavender skies over dreams vast,
Cerulean moments, sweet to last.

Splattered thoughts on canvas wild,
Fragments of whimsy, wonder piled,
Ruby passions, fervent cries,
Emerald hopes beneath sunrise.

Each splash a note in symphony,
With hues of love's deep harmony,
Indigo nights of whispered truth,
Amber days that sing of youth.

Infinite strokes of time's embrace,
In every line, a soulful trace,
Essence captured, splashed in light,
On canvas stretched through day and night.

Textured Whispers

Textures speak in hushed refrain,
Wooden grains or linen plain,
Whispers surface, subtle play,
In tactile night and tender day.

Granite strength in sorrow's song,
Silken seams where hearts belong,
Velvet thoughts in twilight's fold,
Leathered tales in memories old.

Patterns woven, stories spun,
Fabric of life, each thread begun,
In every touch, a whispered gleam,
In textured whispers, hearts redeem.

Fingers trace the lines of time,
In cryptic textures, whispers chime,
Soft or coarsely, tales unfurl,
In every weave, another world.

Infinity in Oils

Infinite strokes on canvas laid,
In oils, love and loss portrayed,
Golden moments, amber sighs,
In vivid hues, each vision lies.

Skies of violet, fields of green,
Oils capture sights unseen,
Sunset fires in crimson red,
Blues unwind where dreams are sped.

Layers build in depth profound,
Where emotions' echoes sound,
Each stroke a glimpse of heart's desire,
In every layer, passion's fire.

Infinite stories in each tone,
In oils, the heart is shown,
On the canvas, life unfurls,
In each brushstroke, a universe swirls.

Chromatic Crescendo

In a realm where colors blend,
The sky unlaces, hues ascend.
Echoes of the twilight send,
Whispers of the sun's descend.

Shades of blue and reds entwine,
In twilight's soft, enchanting line.
Momentary, serene design,
Where earth and heavens redefine.

Harmony in chromatic play,
Dancing lights will never stay.
In delicate twilight's ballet,
Night absorbs the vocal ray.

Seasonal Impressions

Springtime whispers past the dawn,
Blossoms burst where cold has gone.
Nature's palette, brightly drawn,
Life resumes in colors' spawn.

Summer, bold with verdant sea,
Sunlit trails and laughter free.
Golden days that flee in glee,
Skyward eyes and hearts agree.

Autumn's breath on petals kissed,
Crimson leaves and morning mist.
Memories in auburn twist,
Wane the days as sunlight tryst.

Winter weaves a silken white,
Stars embedded in the night.
Silent dreams in frost's delight,
Guardians of fleeting light.

Tinted Soliloquies

In twilight's hush, the colors speak,
A soliloquy for the meek.
Lavender clouds, whispers sleek,
Moments where our worlds peak.

Crimson thoughts in hearts evoke,
Silent dreams in words bespoke.
In each verse, our spirits soak,
In gentle hues, messages cloak.

Amber fades to night's embrace,
In shadows cast, we find our place.
Wisdom in each painted trace,
Guiding us through time's slow pace.

Ephemeral, yet deeply burned,
Lessons in each color turned.
In their silence, truth discerned,
In every hue, secrets learned.

Inkwell's Murmur

Deep in the inkwell, secrets lie,
Stories penned by the silent sky.
In the binding, minds can fly,
To worlds where dreams will never die.

Letters dance in ink's caress,
Quiet thoughts with no duress.
Through the pages words confess,
Life in ink, emotions press.

From each stroke, a tale unfolds,
Timeless, ageless, it beholds.
In every line, the heart consoles,
Truths unspoken it remolds.

Whispers from the quill's embrace,
Illuminate the hidden space.
In inkwell's depth, we find our grace,
Solace in the written trace.

Imprint of Spirit

Within the whisper of the breeze,
A tale of ages past unfolds.
In silent heartbeats it weaves,
A saga the spirit holds.

Footprints on the sands of time,
Etched by souls unseen.
Memories of the climb,
Through realms serene.

Echoes in the twilight,
Soft as morning dew.
In the still of night,
Dreams take flight anew.

Reflections in a tear,
Mirrors of the mind.
In joy and in fear,
The spirit shall unwind.

Journeys through the soul,
Mysterious and deep.
Where the tides of life roll,
And ancient secrets keep.

Creative Harmony

Canvas kissed by color's grace,
Together paint a universe.
Each shade in its place,
Blending in converse.

Brushes dance in unity,
Waltzing across the day.
In strokes of impunity,
Art finds its way.

Melodies in every hue,
Songs within each line.
A symphony that's true,
In pattern and design.

Harmony within the light,
Balance in each space.
Creativity takes flight,
In every painted trace.

Crafting dreams in twilight's gleam,
Mind and heart connect.
In the artist's silent dream,
Perfection they detect.

Essence in Hues

In the palette's varied shades,
Lies the essence of a soul.
Vignettes that time invades,
Making the being whole.

Azure skies on canvas spread,
Echoes of the sea.
Whispers of the dreams ahead,
Laden with mystery.

Crimson portrays passion's heat,
Life's emboldened streak.
Silent, strong and discreet,
In each vibrant peak.

Pastels of the dawn,
Gentle morning light.
In each quiet fawn,
Softness takes its flight.

Hues tell stories untold,
Colors weave the core.
In shades both brave and bold,
The essence they restore.

Painter's Inner Light

Beyond the veil of sight,
Where secrets gently dwell.
Inside a painter's light,
Resides a silent spell.

Every brushstroke breathes,
Whispers of the heart.
In each line, a being seethes,
And artistry takes part.

Light within the darkest shade,
In twilight sings a song.
In the colors softly laid,
Memories belong.

Shadows blend with gleam,
In harmony they play.
In the painter's dream,
Night is turned to day.

Light within the soul confined,
A beacon shining bright.
In the strokes entwined,
Reveals the inner light.

Phantom Landscapes

In misty veils, the mountains rise,
Whispers of ancient, hidden skies.
Rivers flow with silent grace,
Tracing paths in a timeless place.

Shadowed cliffs and valleys deep,
Secrets in the night they keep.
Windswept plains where echoes roam,
Nature's heart, its quiet home.

Where twilight meets the dawn's embrace,
The phantom world reveals its face.
Silent sentinels stand tall,
Guardians of the earth's great hall.

Eclipsed beneath a silver moon,
Forests hum a haunting tune.
Phantom landscapes, ever near,
Drawn from dreams, crystal clear.

A place where time gently bends,
And to the horizon, the dream descends.
In silent awe, the soul beholds,
The phantom landscapes it enfolds.

Colors of Existence

Amber dawn and twilight's hue,
Creation's palette, bold and true.
Emerald forests, oceans blue,
Life expressed in every view.

Golden fields and amber skies,
In them, the universe lies.
Crimson sunsets, soft and deep,
In their warmth, our spirits steep.

In every shade, a story told,
Of life and love, both young and old.
Through prism's dance, a tale unfolds,
Of existence painted in diverse molds.

Azure dreams and silver night,
Scattering stars in soft twilight.
The colors weave through dark and light,
Defining form in pure delight.

In every color, a touch of grace,
A fleeting glimpse of time and space.
The colors of existence gleam,
Reality, a vivid dream.

Mysteries in Pigment

Brush of hues on canvas bare,
Life's deep mysteries resting there.
Layered drapes of shadowed tone,
Stories whisper in the unknown.

Shades of night and bursts of day,
Secrets held in dark and gray.
In pigment's dance, they softly play,
Dreams and fears in bold display.

Silent blues and fervent reds,
Tales of love and hope that threads.
In each stroke, the heart is fed,
Mysteries in pigment spread.

Textures rich with lived intrigue,
Hidden truths in each motif.
Colors blend and patterns league,
In their depths, we seek relief.

By artist's hand, worlds unveil,
Truth and fiction in each trail.
Mysteries in pigment lie,
In their beauty, we espy.

Colors of Existence

Amber dawn and twilight's hue,
Creation's palette, bold and true.
Emerald forests, oceans blue,
Life expressed in every view.

Golden fields and amber skies,
In them, the universe lies.
Crimson sunsets, soft and deep,
In their warmth, our spirits steep.

In every shade, a story told,
Of life and love, both young and old.
Through prism's dance, a tale unfolds,
Of existence painted in diverse molds.

Azure dreams and silver night,
Scattering stars in soft twilight.
The colors weave through dark and light,
Defining form in pure delight.

In every color, a touch of grace,
A fleeting glimpse of time and space.
The colors of existence gleam,
Reality, a vivid dream.

Mysteries in Pigment

Brush of hues on canvas bare,
Life's deep mysteries resting there.
Layered drapes of shadowed tone,
Stories whisper in the unknown.

Shades of night and bursts of day,
Secrets held in dark and gray.
In pigment's dance, they softly play,
Dreams and fears in bold display.

Silent blues and fervent reds,
Tales of love and hope that threads.
In each stroke, the heart is fed,
Mysteries in pigment spread.

Textures rich with lived intrigue,
Hidden truths in each motif.
Colors blend and patterns league,
In their depths, we seek relief.

By artist's hand, worlds unveil,
Truth and fiction in each trail.
Mysteries in pigment lie,
In their beauty, we espy.

Spirit's Canvas

On spirit's canvas, dreams are drawn,
With echoes of the night and dawn.
Whispers of the soul unfold,
In shades both vivid and bold.

Silent strokes of inner thought,
Worlds unseen and battles fought.
In each line, a piece of heart,
Cosmic tales of life impart.

With colors deep and shapes unseen,
It arches through the flowing stream.
A journey weaves in tones serene,
Of realms that lie 'twixt and between.

Spirit's brush, both firm and free,
Paints a realm of mystery.
In every hue, a story's framed,
In every shade, a soul's reclaimed.

Echoes linger on the page,
Boundless tales from age to age.
On spirit's canvas, truth is laid,
Where the fabric of dreams is made.

Vivid Heartbeats

In twilight's gentle embrace,
Through whispers, shadows weave,
Where dreams and fate converge,
In hearts, we still believe.

Colors of the evening sky,
Paint a canvas so profound,
Every hue a story told,
Vivid heartbeats' sound.

Beneath the silence lies,
An echo of the past,
Memories etched in time,
Moments meant to last.

With every pulse, we feel,
A dance of joy and pain,
Vivid heartbeats speak,
Of love's enduring reign.

As twilight fades to night,
In dreams, we find our place,
Vivid heartbeats guide us,
Through life's intricate maze.

Fluid Impressions

Waves upon a silent shore,
Whisper tales untold,
Fluid impressions carved by time,
In sands of purest gold.

Reflections in the water's dance,
Mirrors of the soul,
Each ripple tells a different tale,
Of a world beyond control.

Raindrops on a windowpane,
Like teardrops from the sky,
Fluid impressions on the glass,
As sorrow passes by.

The river flows, unceasing song,
Through valleys deep and wide,
Fluid impressions gently mark,
The ever-changing tide.

In the ebb and flow of life,
We find our transient place,
Fluid impressions of our hearts,
In time's endless embrace.

Pastels of Passion

In hues of softest blush,
A tender story grows,
Pastels of passion softly speak,
Of love that gently flows.

Beneath the colors lies,
A symphony of dreams,
Pastels of passion merge and blend,
In sunlight's golden beams.

A touch of light, a shade of grace,
In every whispered sigh,
Pastels of passion paint the sky,
With love that dares to fly.

Through every storm and serenade,
These colors do persist,
Pastels of passion linger on,
In every lover's kiss.

In quiet moments, hearts connect,
Beyond the world's distraction,
Pastels of passion softly glow,
In love's true reflation.

Sculpting the Intangible

With hands that grasp the fleeting,
We mold the unseen air,
Sculpting the intangible.
In realms beyond compare.

Ideas take form in whispers,
Dreams rise upon the breeze,
Sculpting the intangible,
With effortless ease.

From thoughts to vivid being,
Creations spin and whirl,
Sculpting the intangible,
In a never-ending twirl.

Each sculpture tells a story,
Of mysteries well-kept,
Sculpting the intangible,
With faith that's never slept.

In the space between the stars,
Where countless dreams arise,
Sculpting the intangible,
We bring to life the skies.

Keeping Time in Oil

Brush strokes on canvas wide,
Dreams tangled in the hue,
Minutes merge with tide,
Shades reflect the blue.

Palettes of thought align,
Each one, a story told,
Hours blend, refine,
In colors rich and bold.

Midnight black evolves,
Dawn's light breaks anew,
Mysteries it solves,
In every changing view.

Seasons pass, unhurried,
Oils dance then dry,
Every moment, buried,
In the artist's sly.

Timeless whispers sing,
From canvases aglow,
Captured in a swing,
Where painted rivers flow.

Tints of Life

Rose petals softly sheen,
Spring's first morning light,
Shadows, shades between,
Fold into the night.

Warmth of setting sun,
Calls of dusk it spins,
Echoes, whispers run,
Where twilight begins.

Golden locks of wheat,
Fields that sways as one,
Autumn's kiss is sweet,
Under harvest's sun.

Winter's frosty lace,
Crystals glide and twirl,
Nature's sheer embrace,
In its icy swirl.

Life in hues, a play,
Tones of earth and sky,
Each tint's thoughtful sway,
Blends where hours lie.

Symphony in Paint

Colors form a tune,
Notes in every hue,
Morning, afternoon,
Their orchestra in view.

Brushes write a score,
Lines and dots unite,
Every stroke implores,
A melody in light.

Cadence bright and bold,
Echoes in each vein,
Shades in movements old,
Compose a sweet refrain.

Textures harmonize,
Sync in silent song,
Rhythms in disguise,
On the canvas long.

From dawn till twilight's call,
Artwork takes its flight,
Paintings rise and fall,
In symphony of sight.

Mosaic of Memories

Fragments pieced with care,
Tales of times gone by,
Moments caught in air,
Glimpses never die.

Echoes from the past,
Shattered, yet they shine,
In patterns held fast,
Each shard a sign.

Whispers of old days,
Held in vibrant light,
Stories in a glaze,
Of colors deep and bright.

Borders blend and blur,
Tesserae align,
In the dance they stir,
Past and present bind.

Memories both vast,
Infinite and small,
Within the mosaic cast,
Lives and loves recall.

Crafted Sentiments

Beneath the shade where whispers play,
Words crafted from the heart's array,
Echoes of thoughts in soft relay,
Soft as the night, as light turns gray.

In parchment dreams, our tales unfurl,
In ink, emotions start to swirl,
Crafted lines begin to twirl,
In subtle grace that leaves the pearl.

Each heartbeat writes a silent letter,
In tones that make the soul feel better,
Soft sentiments entwine the tether,
Binding hearts with love's own fetter.

Inked Reflexions

Mirror worlds in ink reveal,
Layers deep of thoughts surreal,
Words in truth that subtly heal,
Wounds within that time conceal.

In every stroke, a story lies,
Of echoed dreams and whispered sighs,
In ink, the truth wears no disguise,
Reflecting what the heart implies.

Pages turn, revealing dreams,
Flowing like the silent streams,
In each line, reflection gleams,
On inked roads, the soul redeems.

Pastel Passions

Soft hues of the pastel dawn,
Where dreams and light are gently drawn,
In tender swirls, our hearts are fawn,
In passion's glow, we're softly gone.

In colors mixed with love's own hand,
Feelings stretch across the sand,
Where oceans meet the dreaming land,
In pastel tones, our spirits stand.

Each shade a chord in love's refrain,
A melody that soothes the pain,
In pastel dreams, we can't remain,
For in this art, we're free again.

Mingling Tones

In melodies that softly ring,
Notes of life begin to sing,
In mingling tones, our hearts take wing,
And to these songs, our souls we bring.

Each harmony a whispered touch,
Connecting lives, meaning much,
In tones that blend, there's love's own clutch,
Holding tight, a gentle such.

Music weaving through each day,
With mingling tones of hope's array,
In every note, our hearts convey,
A love that time will not betray.

Acrylic Dreams

Canvas kissed by morning's glaze,
Brushstrokes dance in vibrant haze,
Colors swirl in fluid streams,
Crafting worlds of acrylic dreams.

Sunsets captured, boundless skies,
Hope adorned in every rise,
Shadows blend with morning beams,
Wondrous tales in acrylic dreams.

Faces formed in careful strokes,
Life ignites where silence cloaks,
Every hue a whispered theme,
Whispered tales of acrylic dreams.

Memories in layers deep,
Waking hearts from dormant sleep,
Boundless beauty, timeless themes,
Living hues of acrylic dreams.

Eyes that gaze beyond the seams,
Awakening in acrylic dreams,
Endless palettes, light that gleams,
Endless art in acrylic dreams.

Pigmented Whispers

Silent murmurs, colors speak,
Hues that brighten dull and bleak,
Tales untold in tender clips,
Echoed soft in pigmented drips.

Nature's voice in pigment's cast,
Timeless whispers from the past,
Every drop a story lisps,
Fading hues, pigmented whispers.

Mountains rise in shades obscure,
Seas of blue, serene and pure,
Every layer, life persists,
Deep within pigmented whispers.

Journeys inked on paper fine,
Travelers through space and time,
Endless paths where wonder trips,
Guided by pigmented whispers.

In the quiet, spectrum's song,
Brushes blend where we belong,
Dreams and hopes in color's grips,
Held close in pigmented whispers.

Inked Reverie

Lines that flow like river's grace,
Moments etched in blackened lace,
In the ink, our hearts set free,
Solitude in inked reverie.

Pages tell of distant shores,
Myths and legends, ancient lore,
Worlds unfold from pen's decree,
Dreaming through inked reverie.

Whispers soft from quills so old,
Thoughts and secrets gently told,
Every mark a silent plea,
Carved within inked reverie.

Letters form like starlit skies,
Boundless realms where spirit flies,
Every word a soul's decree,
Timeless in inked reverie.

Endless night with ink in hand,
Crafting dreams on paper's land,
Life's mosaic, wild and free,
Captured in inked reverie.

Ebony and Ivory

Contrasts blend in monochrome,
Silent keys in light and gloam,
Life's emotions, note by key,
Harmony in ebony and ivory.

Day and night in balanced fall,
Melodies that rise and call,
Songs of old and yet to be,
Played through keys of ebony and ivory.

Stories told in silent might,
Dark and light, both wrong and right,
Every key a mystery,
In the blend of ebony and ivory.

The piano sings of joy and pain,
Silent tears in sweet refrain,
Each note an eternity,
Echoed in ebony and ivory.

Hands that glide with gentle touch,
Crafting symphonies from hush,
In the end, a symphony,
United in ebony and ivory.

Resonance of Hues

In twilight's tender, fleeting light,
Where colors merge, a silent fight,
A spectrum dances, soft, unseen,
In whispers blue and emerald green.

The sky a canvas, dusk's embrace,
Brushstrokes vibrant in their grace,
A symphony of shades in play,
Resonant hues at close of day.

A golden thread through verdant glade,
Glimmers in the evening's fade,
Painted whispers, shadows blend,
In twilight's song, the colors mend.

Where azure dreams and scarlet wane,
A palette born of joy and pain,
A resonant huescape subtly spins,
In every heart the light begins.

Sun's retreat and moon's ascent,
Chasing daylight, pale lament,
Within each echo, color's ruse,
Reside the whispers of the hues.

Evoked in Marble

In marble's cold, eternal breath,
Carved whispers of life, defy death,
A timeless dance in chiseled grace,
Voices still through time and space.

Each glimmered touch, an artist's dream,
Echoes silent, yet they seem,
To breathe the thoughts once set in stone,
In marble's heart, one's soul is known.

Figures poised in pulse and vein,
Silent hymns of joy and pain,
Hands that worked to set them free,
Now in marble, memory.

Grace immortal, cold and bright,
Flame of life in pale moonlight,
Sculpted whispers, stories told,
In evoked marble, art unfolds.

From timeless depth, a silent call,
In every groove, life stands tall,
Evoked in marble, hearts align,
Through stone's embrace, past and divine.

Colorful Echoes

In laughter's burst and sorrow's cue,
Color's echo, bright and true,
In hearts and skies, their whispers ride,
Below the vast, the deep, the wide.

Echoes painted, voices blend,
In vibrant hues that never end,
Each shade a word, a fleeting sound,
In silence, colorful, profound.

From canvas pale, to world alight,
These echoes shimmer in the night,
Brushing whispers, shadows bright,
Within each echo, color's flight.

In every stroke, a memory,
Tone and tint, in symphony,
Life's palette, vast and free,
In echoes vibrant, we can see.

Moments caught, in prisms lie,
In colorful echoes, we find the sky,
Bright reflections, voices new,
Color's echoes, fresh and true.

Inner Worlds Unpainted

Within the quiet, yet unseen,
Lies worlds untold and evergreen,
Soft whispers hum where shadows lie,
Inner realms none can defy.

Unpainted visions, dreams unfold,
A canvas vast, by none controlled,
In silent corners thoughts arise,
Inner worlds through hidden eyes.

Brush untouched, yet colors blend,
In shadowed realms where dreams descend,
Unseen landscapes, vast and wide,
Whispered secrets, deep inside.

Journeys taken, none can trace,
Inward flights through boundless space,
Unpainted dreams in silent flight,
Inner worlds in darkest night.

Mystic realms within us all,
Silent, deep, yet soft they call,
Unpainted, yet in whispers bright,
Inner worlds that grace our sight.

Vision in Varnish

The brush caresses silent tales,
Across the canvas, colors sail,
A dance of hues that never fails,
In visions varnished, all details.

A spectrum born in twilight's kiss,
Unfurling dreams that swirl and twist,
Where life is painted, not amiss,
In varnished vision's tender mist.

Each stroke whispers ancient lore,
Of love and loss, of peace and war,
Through varnish, scenes forever more,
A silent witness to explore.

In every hue, a story blends,
From start to never-ending ends,
A painter's soul, a friend that lends,
Varnished visions, heart contends.

By candlelight, the colors gleam,
Reflecting dusk's elusive dream,
Visions in varnish, like a stream,
Of art's eternal, living theme.

Radiant Chapters

In gilded tomes where sunbeams rest,
With pages kissed by nature's zest,
Each word a star, a radiant quest,
In chapters glowing, hearts are blessed.

Fables spun in twilight's glow,
In radiant chapters, stories grow,
Of heroes bold and love's sweet flow,
In paths where dreams and sunlight show.

Through ancient scripts and songs of lore,
We journey far through every door,
With radiant chapters, we explore,
And find where souls can soar and more.

The ink that binds our past and now,
Weaves futures bright upon its brow,
Chapters radiant, teach us how,
To live in light, not just allow.

So turn the pages, let them sing,
Of radiant chapters blossoming,
In every moment, life will bring,
A tale of hope, a brightening.

Figure and Form

In shadowed curves and gentle lines,
The form reveals what's undefined,
A figure poised, in art confines,
Yet boundless in the heart and mind.

A symphony in marble's grace,
In every curve, the soul we trace,
From figure and form, a warm embrace,
Eternal beauty, time can't erase.

The sculptor's hand, with tender touch,
Brings forth a muse from stone and such,
In form and figure, love is much,
More than the eye, a feeling's clutch.

Through chisel's edge, creation blooms,
In studio's quiet, hallowed rooms,
Figures and forms ignite the flumes,
Where art transforms, the heart consumes.

In every pose, a life's refrain,
In form and figure, joy and pain,
A testament that will remain,
Of human touch, in art's domain.

Echoes on Canvas

Beneath the sky where colors play,
The echoes on canvas silently stay,
A whisper of dawn, a night's soft fray,
In painted echoes, hearts convey.

Each brushstroke captures fleeting breath,
Moments of life defying death,
In echoes on canvas, tales of depth,
Where memories reside and gently crept.

A glance, a scene, a silent cry,
With every hue, with every sigh,
On canvas spread beneath the sky,
Echoes of moments passing by.

Through texture and through shadow's game,
Life's fleeting pulse is not the same,
In echoes on canvas, framed by name,
A timeless dance of light and flame.

So let the colors speak in streams,
Of distant pasts and closer dreams,
Echoes on canvas, like moonbeams,
Reflecting life in silent gleams.

Rhythms of the Palette

In vibrant hues and shadows cast,
The artist's hand moves brisk and fast,
A world of color on a canvas vast,
Each stroke a memory meant to last.

Cadmium red and cobalt blue,
Blend together, something new,
The heart and soul in every hue,
A dance of pigments, bold and true.

Brushes trace the beat of time,
Creating patterns so sublime,
In every layer, a hidden rhyme,
Rhythms flow in art's grand prime.

Emerald green, sienna raw,
Draw the eye to nature's law,
Capturing moments that leave in awe,
The palette's rhythm, without a flaw.

A symphony of light and shade,
Where dreams and reality fade,
In each bold stroke that's carefully laid,
Art's true essence is displayed.

Echoes in Cerulean

Beneath the sky so vast and wide,
Cerulean whispers side by side,
Echoes of dreams we often hide,
Flowing like the ocean's tide.

In waves of blue, our thoughts align,
Translucent whispers intertwine,
Mysteries in the depths combine,
In cerulean's endless sign.

Azure skies and sapphire seas,
Carry whispers in the breeze,
A canvas of the soul's decrees,
Echoes found in tranquil pleas.

Softly hums the twilight air,
Cerulean beyond compare,
Each note a breath of beauty rare,
In echoes found, the heart laid bare.

Through the veils of time and space,
Cerulean's touch leaves a trace,
An echo of a timeless grace,
In its embrace, our spirits chase.

Dreams in Strokes

Dreams unfold with each sweet line,
In strokes of color, they define,
A secret world of bright design,
Where hopes and visions intertwine.

In whispers soft, the pigments tell,
Of dreams that in the silence dwell,
On canvas seen, their stories swell,
With every stroke, they weave a spell.

Brushes dip in hues profound,
Creating realms where dreams are found,
Silent echoes, without sound,
In strokes that make the heart rebound.

From twilight hues to dawn's embrace,
In every stroke, a fleeting grace,
Dreams take form in this quiet space,
Colors capturing time's swift pace.

Upon the canvas, dreams arise,
In strokes of love, beneath the skies,
A tapestry of truths and lies,
Painted in the artist's eyes.

Pigments of Emotion

Colors swirl, a tempest wild,
Emotions painted, undefiled,
In every drop, a heart beguiled,
Pigments speak where words are mild.

Red of passion, blue of sorrow,
Each hue tells of a time we borrow,
In the mix, our joys and woe,
In pigments deep, emotions flow.

Yellow light of hope's embrace,
Green of envy leaves its trace,
In every stroke, a hidden face,
Emotions blend in art's soft grace.

Purple dreams of twilight's kiss,
Emotions tangle, twist in bliss,
The artist's heart in pigments miss,
A world of feelings in abyss.

Canvas holds the silent cries,
In colors where the spirit flies,
Emotions marked in vibrant dyes,
Art's true voice never lies.

Visual Poetry

In frames of gold, the visions play,
Brushes dance with colors bold.
Each stroke a verse on canvas lay,
An artist's song in hues unfold.

With light and shadow's tender grace,
A tale in pigments softly told.
Beyond the edges, dreams embrace,
A world of wonder to behold.

Blue whispers of a twilight's kiss,
Orange flames of dawn's embrace.
In silken shades of muted bliss,
Emotions painted on the face.

The whispers in the gallery,
Silent sonnets, dreams displayed.
Ephemeral yet evergreen,
A timeless beauty never swayed.

Lines of Life

Threads that weave through time and space,
Tapestries of joy and strife.
In each line, the heart we trace,
Every moment, beats of life.

Verses etched on pages old,
Stories in the wrinkles, seams.
In the quiet, tales unfold,
In shadows cast by moonlit beams.

In laughter's echo, sorrow's sigh,
Lives entwined, like vines they grow.
Through the fabric, bold and shy,
A dance of highs and undertows.

In the pulse of every morn,
And the twilight's tender glow.
Lines of life are drawn in form,
To the end, and still they flow.

Vibrant Connections

In the web of threads we spin,
Destinies and hearts entwined.
Connections vibrant, deep within,
Mirrors of the soul defined.

Through veils of time and distant lands,
Silent echoes call us near.
In the meeting of clasped hands,
We find we're far, yet always here.

Flashes of a knowing glance,
Shared rhythms in a breath.
In the weave of life's great dance,
We touch the vast, sidestep death.

A spectrum's arc in fleeting touch,
Colors blend and lives align.
A brushstroke here, a swirl as such,
Vibrant connections intertwine.

Acrylic Reveries

Upon the easel's humble throne,
Dreams are rendered pure and bright.
In layers thick, emotions prone,
A spectrum's dance in morning light.

A brush dipped in the twilight's sigh,
Sweeps of skies in bold array.
Acrylic whispers, hues imply,
A world reborn with each new day.

In abstract forms and simple lines,
Reflections of the heart and mind.
In every curve, the soul defines,
A vivid path for eyes to find.

Beyond the frame, in vivid streams,
The painter's heart and hand explore.
A realm where waking meets with dreams,
Acrylic reveries implore.

Ethereal Shades

Beneath the canvas of the twilight sky,
Where gentle whispers of the zephyrs sigh,
Shadows dance in luminous cascade,
Within the realm of ethereal shade.

Softly lingers the twilight glow,
Embracing whispers from aeons ago,
Colors blend in hues surreal,
Creating dreams that feel so real.

Stars like diamonds in velvet gleam,
Woven in a cosmic, silent dream,
Mysteries in the night parade,
Painting life in ethereal shade.

Moonlight spills its silver beams,
Awaking ancient lore and schemes,
Underneath this tranquil serenade,
Hearts find rest in ethereal shade.

Visions Unveiled

Within the mind, a tapestry weaves,
Of stories spun through countless eves,
Secrets hidden, softly hailed,
In a realm of visions unveiled.

Light and shadow merge and sway,
Revealing paths that dreams convey,
Through misty veils and star-lit trails,
Guiding spirits on their sails.

Ancient echoes softly call,
Beneath the heavens' endless sprawl,
Guardian whispers never failed,
Keeping souls with visions unveiled.

At dawn's embrace, the truth unfolds,
In colors bright and warmth so bold,
A world where magic has prevailed,
And life itself, through visions unveiled.

Dreamscapes in Color

In the hush of midnight hours,
Dreams bloom like unseen flowers,
Bathing in a rainbow's hue,
Crafting realms no soul yet knew.

Auroras paint the skies so vast,
Blending memories from the past,
Each stroke a story to uncover,
Within these dreamscapes in color.

Softly whispering through the night,
Stars reflect an inner light,
Journeying through a canvas of more,
Beyond the realms we've known before.

In dreams, our spirits learn to soar,
To vistas, wild, and ever more,
A spectrum of emotions hover,
In this place, dreamscapes in color.

Imagination's Touch

In the stillness of a fleeting thought,
Wonders greater than we sought,
Flourish with a gentle brush,
Crafted by imagination's touch.

Worlds within a single glance,
Where dreams and fancies freely dance,
Limitless as stars above,
Inspired by an endless love.

Notes of wonder, free and wild,
As they sing; our hearts beguiled,
Creativity begins to rush,
Flowing from imagination's touch.

In whispers of the wind, it's found,
Echoes speaking all around,
Hearts and minds in wondrous hush,
Awaken to imagination's touch.

Abstract Reflections

Twisting forms and shapeless dreams,
In a world where nothing's as it seems,
Brushstrokes wild, untamed, and free,
Echoing abstract harmony.

Colors clash and dance around,
In chaos, beauty can be found,
Every line and curve a quest,
Seeking meaning never guessed.

Circles, squares, and lines so sharp,
Each a fragment of the heart,
Lost in thought, they intertwine,
In patterns rich, they redefine.

Silent whispers in the dark,
Touch a soul, ignite the spark,
In the abstract's bold embrace,
Reflections find their hidden place.

In a canvas, broad and wide,
Where emotions need not hide,
Abstract reflections deeply pour,
Unlocking dreams to deeply explore.

Impressions of the Mind

In silent whispers of the night,
Thoughts take wing, take flight,
Impressions vivid, abstract line,
Trace the contours of the mind.

Dreams and visions, softly sway,
In a dance where shadows play,
Figures shifting, forming new,
Impressions rich with every hue.

Gentle waves of thought arise,
In the deep of closed eyes,
Every breath a new design,
Crafted in the depths of mind.

Voices echo, faint yet clear,
In the stillness, they appear,
Weaving tales unseen, unshown,
In the mind's vast, silent throne.

Every thought, a fleeting brush,
Painting in the quiet hush,
Impressions linger, softly twined,
Patterns in the vast of mind.

Da Vinci's Muse

Oh, da Vinci, tell me true,
What inspired strokes from you?
Genius, whispers on the breeze,
Musing through the olive trees.

Silken threads of history,
Woven deep in mystery,
Figures rise from shadows drawn,
In the light of breaking dawn.

Mona Lisa's secret smile,
Captures hearts across the miles,
Eyes that follow, soft yet wise,
Windows deep where soul lies.

Inventions birthed from dreams aloft,
Sketches tender, lines so soft,
Imagination's grand delight,
Soaring high in boundless flight.

Da Vinci's muse, eternal flame,
Legacy, enduring name,
Art and science, intertwined,
In his works, forever shined.

Prismatic Meditations

In prisms' dance, the colors blend,
Through soft beams light ascend,
A tranquil mind in hues so gentle,
Thoughts arise, transcendental.

Whispers of a dawn unfound,
Echoes in a silent sound,
Dreams in vibrant spectrum swim,
Stillness found on daylight's rim.

Rainbows arch above the haze,
Reflecting on the soul's gaze,
In meditative, peaceful trance,
To nature's song, we dance.

Ephemeral, the moments pass,
Like dew upon the morning grass,
Colors fade, but mem'ries linger,
In the heart, a softest whisper.

Crystalline in light's embrace,
Find the calm, a sacred place,
Where thought becomes a river's flow,
In prismatic lights, we grow.

Harmony in Hues

In twilight's gentle, purple glow,
Where golden sunbeams cease to show,
Colors blend in dusky trance,
Nature's canvas, perfect dance.

Emerald greens turn deep and dark,
Meeting blues where night embarks,
Crimson blushes, warm and bright,
Fade to shadows in moonlight.

Amber streaks in sky so wide,
Mingle softly, side by side,
Brush of wind and whispers soft,
Lift the palette high aloft.

Silent symphonies that play,
Beneath the stars' soft array,
Every stroke in calm repose,
Harmony in hues disclose.

In this vast, expansive space,
Colors merge with gentle grace,
Painting night in tones so true,
Harmony in every hue.

Fragmented Thoughts

In fragments of a moonlit night,
Pieces scatter out of sight,
Wandering a mind at drift,
Waves that crest, and currents shift.

Memory shards, a scattered gleam,
Suspended in a waking dream,
Grasping moments, fleeting fast,
Fragments in a shadow cast.

It's not the whole but part we see,
In fleeting thought and reverie,
A mosaic of what's nearly known,
Stories etched in heart and bone.

Splintered light through cracked façade,
Shows the beauty of the flawed,
In fragments find a sense replete,
An incomplete that feels complete.

Ghosts of whispers, echoes trace,
In shattered moments find our grace,
Fragmented thoughts, like stars in skies,
Guide us though the night complies.

.

Radiant Musings

In a sunbeam's golden hold,
Stories of the cosmos told,
Seeds of thought in brilliance lay,
Dawn unveils a brighter day.

From the heart, the rays outpour,
Illuminating folklore,
Wisps of dreams and whispered lore,
In radiant musings, soar.

Celestial light in artist's hand,
Paints the sky and sea, the land,
Words like stardust in the air,
Glimmering with tender care.

In each ray, a life's refrain,
Echoes softly, sweet sustain,
Musings that ignite the mind,
In the warmth, the truth we find.

Golden hues of twilight blend,
Musings that with daylight end,
In radiant glow, the soul's dress,
Veiled in light, in soft caress.

Sculpture of Feelings

In marble curves the heart reveals,
Every trace of joy it feels,
Chiseled thoughts and hardened clay,
Sculpt a life in vast array.

Each emotion, deeply etched,
In veins of stone, our stories stretched,
With hammer's strike and artist's will,
Feelings carved, a moment still.

In tender lines and bold embrace,
The sculpture holds a timeless grace,
Every chisel marks the way,
Of hearts once lost and led astray.

In shadows cast by sculptor's hands,
A dance of light, the soul expands,
Eternal forms of love and pain,
Captured in the stone's domain.

The sculpture stands through time's caress,
A monument to life's express,
In frozen forms, the truth is found,
Feelings cast in stone profound.

Kaleidoscope of Thought

In the maze of mirrored glass,
Colors twist and swiftly pass,
Shards of memories, shadows cast,
Whispering tales from the past.

Ideas spin, a vibrant dance,
In the spectrum of a glance,
Fragments form in bright expanse,
A mosaic's fleeting chance.

Dreams unfurl in fractured light,
Thoughts intertwine in dazzling flight,
Patterns shift from dark to bright,
In the kaleidoscope of night.

Magic weaves in crystal glow,
Uncharted realms begin to show,
Endless vistas, thoughts bestow,
In this ever-changing show.

Mind's horizons wide and vast,
Every moment, unsurpassed,
In the shards where truths amassed,
Kaleidoscope of thought, steadfast.

Palette of Serenity

Azure skies in gentle hue,
Soft pastels where dreams are true,
Whispers of the morning dew,
In a world made fresh and new.

Meadows green with tender grace,
Brushstrokes blend in nature's space,
Quiet moments we embrace,
In this tranquil, timeless place.

Sunset shades in amber glow,
Silent rivers cease to flow,
Evening stars begin to show,
In the twilight's sacred glow.

Gentle breezes, lullaby,
Colors of the wind's soft sigh,
Painting peace across the sky,
In the calm where spirits fly.

On this palette, soft and bright,
Find your solace in the light,
In serenity's pure sight,
Worlds of peace in joyous flight.

Textures of the Soul

Canvas deep with hidden threads,
Stories where the heart is led,
Woven whispers, softly said,
Secrets in the soul are spread.

Layers thick with life's embrace,
Each a memory, time's trace,
Every touch, a gentle grace,
In the fabric of this place.

Echoes of a distant song,
Felt within where spirits long,
Textures rough and soft belong,
In the blend where hearts grow strong.

Brush of sorrow, stroke of love,
Tales below, and skies above,
In the weave, emotions shove,
Textures of the soul thereof.

Feel the depths where we define,
Every thread, a sacred line,
In the soul's design divine,
Textures flow, intertwine.

Layers of Expression

Words upon the canvas spilled,
Thoughts and feelings, gently filled,
Layers of emotion stilled,
In the heart where dreams are willed.

Hidden meanings, shadows play,
Depths of what we cannot say,
Every brush, a line of gray,
In the art of night and day.

Expressed in colors, bold and bright,
Truths revealed in silent light,
Every tone, an inner sight,
In the depths, our souls ignite.

Subtle shades of sorrow's tale,
Joy in patterns, soft and frail,
In the layers, we prevail,
Drawing strength from every trail.

Art of heart and mind confessed,
In the layers, we are blessed,
Every stroke, a soul addressed,
Expressions deep, in art's caress.

Spectral Symphony

In twilight's gentle, fading hue,
The notes of night begin to play,
A symphony of shadows true,
As daylight quietly slips away.

The moon conducts with silver wand,
Stars twinkle in harmonious flair,
A dance upon the twilight pond,
Where whispers float and mingle there.

An owl hoots a deep, low note,
Leaves rustle in the evening's croon,
Crickets join with chirps that float,
Beneath the tender light of moon.

This spectral song of night unfolds,
In colors unseen by the day,
As hush envelops, dream enfolds,
In silent night's melodic sway.

A serenade to soft embrace,
The world in lullabies confined,
In spectral symphony, we trace,
The boundless reaches of the mind.

Dappled Thoughts

Beneath the trees where shadows lie,
In patches of the fleeting light,
Thoughts meander, float, and fly,
In dances that escape the night.

Whispers of the wind convey,
Fragments of the dreams unseen,
In the gentle sway, they play,
Creating moments in between.

Sunlight filters, dapples ground,
A myriad of shapes and shades,
In these visions, thoughts are found,
As the afternoon light fades.

Impressions left in patterned lines,
Scattered thoughts like autumn leaves,
In the silence, heart refines,
And the mind in peace believes.

A gallery of dappled dreams,
Painted by the sun and air,
Where nothing truly is, it seems,
But everything is real and rare.

Golden Visions

In the hush of dawn's first light,
Gold spreads across the waking sky,
Painting dreams in hues so bright,
As morning whispers soft and shy.

Fields of amber, waves of grain,
In the sunlight's tender touch,
Golden visions dance, remain,
In the heart that loves so much.

Pebbles gleam in golden stream,
Catching rays of day's bright start,
Flowing through a painted dream,
Warmed by light, refreshed in heart.

A cascade of golden threads,
Weaving tales of ancient lore,
In each strand, a journey spreads,
From past to future's golden door.

Forever caught in golden glow,
These visions, timeless, carry on,
In every dawn, a promise, shown,
Golden dreams that kiss the dawn.

Evanescent Echoes

In the valleys of the mind,
Echoes of a time long past,
Whispered memories, soft, refined,
Echoes fade, yet dreams still last.

Through corridors of ancient thought,
Footsteps gentle on the air,
Phantoms of the past are caught,
In shadows neither here nor there.

Evanescent tales unfold,
In the twilight's fleeting grace,
Stories of the young and old,
In time's tender, soft embrace.

Whispers carried on the breeze,
From voices lost in yesteryears,
Through the silence of the trees,
Their wisdom whispers, calms our fears.

In echoes that surmise the past,
The fleeting moments still remain,
In hearts these memories last,
Evanescent, yet they sustain.

Brushstrokes of Eternity

In the quiet dawn's embrace,
Where time and light entwine,
Brushstrokes paint an endless space,
Aether turns divine.

Through the canvas of the skies,
Stars begin to gleam,
Eternal whispers softly rise,
Merging with the dream.

Mountains etched in twilight hues,
Rivers serpentine,
Nature's palette gently strews,
Moments crystalline.

Colors fade, the day retreats,
Night spreads its serene,
In those strokes, our hearts it meets,
We in peace convene.

On this tapestry so vast,
Life and art unite,
Brushstrokes of eternity cast,
Deep into the night.

Whispers in Color

Hues of dawn begin to speak,
Whispers soft as dew,
Through the mists they gently peak,
Vivid shades accrue.

On the winds the colors fly,
Secrets softly weave,
Nature's dream beneath the sky,
Patterns they conceive.

Whispers in the forest dense,
Emerald leaves that gleam,
In the streams where colors sense,
Mirrors of a dream.

Petals brush in silent dance,
Wind and flowers play,
Whispers in the sunlit trance,
Turn the night to day.

Morning breaks with tender light,
Pastels softly blend,
Whispers in color take flight,
In the heart they send.

Canvas of the Heart

In the canvas of the heart,
Memories take hold,
Every stroke a work of art,
Stories to be told.

Dreams in bright and shadowed hues,
Lines that gently flow,
As the artist gently views,
Where emotions go.

Love is painted golden bright,
Sorrows in the blue,
Passions burning in the night,
Evermore renew.

Canvas stretched in tender care,
Colors intertwine,
Echoes held in moments rare,
As our lives align.

In the quiet of the soul,
Art finds its pure part,
Brushstrokes make the heart a whole,
Masterpiece of heart.

Shades of Inner Light

In the depths of silent night,
Shades of inner glow,
Illuminate with gentle light,
Paths where dreams will go.

Whispers in the starlit veil,
Cast a gentle gleam,
On the waters smooth and pale,
Reflections of a dream.

Moonlight dances on the leaves,
Silver threads unwind,
Nighttime weaves, the heart receives,
Beauty hard to find.

Shades of thought in deepest dark,
Soul begins to heal,
In the shadows soft and stark,
Truths they do reveal.

Inner light, a lantern bright,
Guides the weary way,
Shades of hope in silent night,
Usher in the day.

Immutable Sketches

In whispers old, the canvas lies,
With echoes drawn in fragile lines,
Each stroke a memory, softly wise,
A timeless dance where beauty shines.

An artist's hand, with care, does trace,
The fleeting glance of morning dew,
Preserving moments, time can't erase,
In shadows cast, the sketch renews.

Season's hues blend and unfurl,
In silken threads of twilight's glow,
Drawing the winds, in timeless swirl,
A whispered tale, an ancient show.

Through shifting light, the scenes unfold,
A portrait of eternity,
In lines of ink, a story told,
Immutable in constancy.

Across the years, the figures stand,
Unmoved by fate's uncaring reach,
Immutable sketches, deftly planned,
Within the silence, they still teach.

Echoes in Etching

Upon the stone, a hand does carve,
The echoes of an age gone by,
With every line, the time they starve,
In etchings bold, beneath the sky.

The chisel sings a note of grace,
In rhythmic beats, on granite face,
Whispered legacies, we trace,
In ancient crypts, where shadows race.

Each echo holds a secret voice,
In marble halls, they softly speak,
Resonating past the silent choice,
To seek the truth that time does leak.

In labyrinths of etched design,
The mind does wander, thoughts align,
Finding whispers, deeply twined,
In echoes carved through ageless sign.

Across the eons, etchings last,
In silent testimony still,
A bridge between the future, past,
Where echoes in etching, whispers fill.

Unveiled Mirages

In deserts wide, the visions bloom,
Mirages dance in heat's embrace,
A fleeting glimpse through noon's perfume,
Unveiled by mirth in time and space.

The shimmering light distorts the view,
Of oases green, in sands of gold,
A phantasm past the dunes, in queue,
Whispers of secrets, stories retold.

Each peak and valley, falsely weaves,
A tapestry of dreams unspoken,
As twilight's breath begins to heave,
The mirage fades, the spell broken.

Yet in the heart, the visions cling,
Unveiled in moments, slightly clear,
A promise held in desert's ring,
Of hidden truths, forever near.

Through endless sands, the wanderer chases,
The unveiled mirages, near and far,
Guided by what the mind embraces,
In phantom lights, a guiding star.

Imaginary Quilts

Threads of silver, threads of gold,
Weave the dreams in night's embrace,
Imaginary quilts unfold,
In patterns rich, the stars we chase.

The moonlight spills on woven thread,
Crafting tales from fabric bright,
In each patch, a story spread,
In whispered hues of twilight night.

Softly stitched with thoughts and dreams,
The quilt of life lies intricately,
Imaginary, yet so it seems,
It blankets time in gentle plea.

Each square a world unto itself,
Of hopes and fears, of joy and tears,
A quilt that folds upon the shelf,
Embroidered through the passing years.

In every dream, a quilt is spun,
Imaginary, yet real in heart,
Holding warmth until the dawn has come,
When dreams and reality, do part.

Frescoes of Feeling

In the corridors of ancient halls,
Feelings painted on the walls.
Emotions blend in vivid hues,
Each a story, each a muse.

Brush strokes dance in silent glee,
Tales of sorrow, joy, and sea.
Every fresco, a timeless keeper,
Of the heart's deep, secret sleeper.

From pain to love, the spectrum's wide,
Caverns where our spirits hide.
Art becomes the mirror's grace,
Reflecting every hidden face.

Each pigment tells a silent tale,
In whispers soft, in voices frail.
Yet strong enough to echo past,
A testament meant to last.

So bask within these painted dreams,
Where nothing is quite as it seems.
Frescoes of feeling, bold and bright,
Bathed in the softest, ancient light.

Emotion in Fresco

On a canvas vast and wide,
Emotions spill and cannot hide.
Colors blend in mystic flow,
Capturing what hearts won't show.

Each shade a whisper of the soul,
Fragments making up the whole.
Eyes transfixed, a silent prayer,
In frescoes, love and pain lay bare.

Layered deep with tender care,
Moment's freeze mid solemn stare.
Faces etched in silent screams,
Or lost in sweetest, tender dreams.

The artist's hand, a magic wand,
Weaving worlds in bondless fond.
In every stroke, a heart's confess,
In fresco lies our purest bless.

Gaze upon the wall's embrace,
Find your story, find your place.
Emotion captured, still yet free,
A frescoed world of you and me.

Texture of Thought

In the loom of cosmic thread,
Ideas from the mind are spread.
Textures rich in velvet deep,
In silent corners where they keep.

Patterns born from nights alone,
Intricacies of flesh and bone.
Thoughts unfold in tender weave,
Mesmerizing, make-believe.

Across the fabric thoughts are sown,
Whispers of the heart unknown.
Each little thread a different tale,
A fleeting thought, a timeless gale.

The texture, woven soft and bright,
Mirrors mind in spectral light.
Patterns etched in careful brush,
Textures speaking in the hush.

Feel the thoughts under your skin,
Textures whispering within.
In every thread the world is caught,
Unraveling the texture of thought.

The Sculptor's Vision

In marble blocks, the vision sleeps,
A soul within the stone it keeps.
The sculptor's hands, both firm and sure,
Reveal what lies in granite pure.

With each strike, a shape appears,
Carving through the hidden fears.
A figure forms, a life unknown,
Born from heart and chisel's tone.

Veins of stone and veins of life,
Merge as one in chosen strife.
An artist's dream, a holy quest,
To render truth in form's behest.

The chisel's kiss, both soft and bold,
Turns mere stone to flecks of gold.
Eyes that see beyond the vein,
Craft the perfect, shunned from pain.

Thus stands the vision, pure and clear,
A silent song for all who hear.
The sculptor's heart in every curve,
A love immortal, steel of nerve.

Sketches of Memory

Whispers of time in shadowed hue,
Echoes of laughter long and true.
Faint impressions, silent yet strong,
A dance of memory, where we belong.

Pastel moments on canvas unfurled,
Stories told of another world.
Gentle strokes reveal the past,
In fleeting glimpses, shadows cast.

Wistful glances, a faded smile,
Captured moments that span a mile.
In each line, there's a tale to tell,
A whisper of where our hearts dwell.

Charcoal sketches of days gone by,
Soft reminders of reasons why.
Time's fragile threads weave our tale,
In memory's art, we prevail.

Gentle hands that trace the line,
Sketches of moments, forever mine.
In every mark, a whisper is spun,
Tales of memory, one by one.

Brush with Passion

Painted whispers on canvas lay,
Colors blend in a fiery display.
Bold and vibrant, the strokes do speak,
A brush with passion, ever unique.

Reds and yellows, a blazing sun,
In every stroke, emotions run.
Love and fury, in hues so bright,
A dance of colors in the night.

Textures rich in layered grace,
A symphony in each traced space.
Every movement ignites a spark,
A world created from the dark.

Fiery tones that blaze and burn,
With each brushstroke, passions churn.
A tempest born in shades so deep,
In art's embrace, emotions seep.

Blazing hearts on canvas spread,
Echoed whispers in crimson red.
A brush with passion, fierce and true,
Colors merge in a vibrant view.

Strokes of Infinity

In an endless blue, the strokes begin,
A journey vast, where dreams blend in.
Celestial dances with every line,
In strokes of infinity, stars align.

A void of silence, serene and deep,
In cosmic waves, our secrets keep.
Galaxies formed with a single brush,
In timeless space, a whisper's hush.

Infinite patterns in endless flight,
Nebulae blaze in the darkened night.
Orbits traced in swirling hues,
The universe within, old and new.

Born of mystery in cosmic rhyme,
Strokes that transcend the bounds of time.
Eternal echoes in every shade,
In the vastness of space, art is laid.

Infinity in each expanse so grand,
With every stroke, dreams are planned.
An endless journey in a cosmic sea,
In strokes of infinity, we see.

Chromatic Fantasies

In a twilight world of endless shades,
A realm where each hue never fades.
Chromatic dreams in vibrant spree,
We weave our fantasies, wild and free.

Lavender skies in twilight's hold,
Emerald forests, tales untold.
Ochre fields in golden light,
A symphony of chromatic night.

Palette rich in dreams so grand,
Every color guided by hand.
A realm where imagination flies,
Through chromatic fantasies' skies.

Tangerine mornings and sapphire seas,
A harmony in every breeze.
In each stroke, a story we find,
Colorful dreams in heart and mind.

A painted world in hues so bright,
Chromatic fantasies take flight.
In every shade, a dream unfolds,
Within this world, our hearts behold.

Ink and Inner Fire

In the silence of the night,
Where the moon casts a pale light,
Thoughts like embers ignite,
Burning with a poet's might.

Lines crafted with desire,
On parchment they conspire,
To set the soul afire,
With words that never tire.

Each stroke of ink, a spark,
Brightening the deepest dark,
Tracing tales that leave a mark,
In lore's eternal arc.

Flames of fervor ascend high,
Reaching for the endless sky,
Every verse, a heartfelt sigh,
In ink, dreams learned to fly.

Here, the inner fire feeds,
On whispered hopes and bygone deeds,
Springing forth in earnest needs,
To grow from paper's seeds.

Pigments of Being

In the palette of our days,
Colors blend in mystic ways,
Through the shadows and the rays,
Life's rich tapestry displays.

Bright and bold, the yellows beam,
Casting light on every dream,
In the river's gentle stream,
Reflections of a golden theme.

Deep and somber, hues of blue,
Whisper secrets old and new,
In their depths, a world askew,
Where the heart can find its view.

Reds ignite with passion's fire,
Burning with an intense desire,
In their blaze, we never tire,
Chasing sparks that never expire.

Green and brown, the earth's embrace,
Grounding us in nature's grace,
Roots in place, yet thoughts we chase,
In pigments, our essence trace.

Shadows of Expression

Upon the canvas white and bare,
Brush in hand, with utmost care,
Shadows dance, a gentle flare,
Telling tales of hearts laid bare.

Strokes of grey, so subtly fine,
Weave a story, line by line,
In the twilight, they combine,
Symbols of the soul's design.

Figures formed in twilight's clasp,
Hold the dreams we dare to grasp,
In their midst, emotions rasp,
Silent in their whispered gasp.

Each soft edge, a fleeting trace,
Of a moment, time's embrace,
In the dark, they find their place,
Eclipsed by light, they interlace.

Shadows, cloaked in veiled attire,
Kindling the artist's fire,
In their depth, inspired desire,
Echoes of expression's choir.

Hearts in Watercolor

In the realm of color's play,
Where hues blend and gently sway,
Hearts inscribed in soft array,
Blooming in the light of day.

Blues that wash like ocean's tide,
Softly whisper, gently guide,
To the places where we hide,
Depths where tender feelings bide.

Pinks that blush with life's embrace,
Caressing every hidden space,
In each shade, we find a trace,
Of love's warm, unworn grace.

Greens that heal with nature's balm,
In their calm, our spirits calm,
Every stroke a soothing psalm,
Bringing peace like breeze's palm.

Watery edges blur and blend,
In each heart, the colors send,
Messages that a soul will mend,
With the beauty they attend.

Visionary Stitches

Threads of imagination twist and twine,
Patterns emerging with every line,
Crafting tales in fabric's embrace,
Each stitch a journey through time and space.

Colors whisper secrets under the light,
Hands weaving dreams through the night,
In silent symphony, creativity sways,
A tapestry of unexpected ways.

Glimpses of future, fragments of past,
In every needle's shadow cast,
A stitch for love, a stitch for sorrow,
Binding today with tomorrow.

The needle pauses, the thread takes flight,
In cloth, visions burn bright,
With each pull, a world rewinds,
Stories stitched in elaborate designs.

Moments etched in every seam,
Threads of reality, threads of dream,
Art emerges, gentle and grand,
In the palm of the visionary's hand.

Hearts on Canvas

Brush strokes dance on a blank expanse,
In colors bold, emotions enhance,
A heart revealed in every hue,
Passion painted pure and true.

Canvas breathes with every stroke,
Layers of love they soon evoke,
Silent whispers in vibrant scenes,
Heartfelt stories in reds and greens.

Textures rich with joy and pain,
A soulful rhythm, a sweet refrain,
Each line, a pulse, each curve, a sigh,
Love immortalized, suspended in the sky.

Shades of twilight, splashes of dawn,
A heartlier language together drawn,
Brushes share what words may miss,
In painted embrace, an eternal kiss.

Creations bloom in vivid flair,
Eternal, though fragile, though rare,
Every color, an emotion alive,
In the canvas where lovers strive.

Mosaic of Mirrors

Shards of glass, reflections break,
A mosaic of memories we tend to make,
Each piece a flicker of who we are,
In mirrored fragments near and far.

Light refracts in splinters bright,
Crafting patterns in the dark of night,
Faces change as angles twist,
Past and present coexist.

Mirrored realms in perfect shards,
Dreams and truths their surface guards,
In every crack a story lies,
Mosaic worlds beneath our eyes.

Prisms hold the light we seek,
Timeless echoes where fragments speak,
Images flowing, ever redefined,
Mirrors reflecting soul and mind.

A unity forged in broken parts,
Piece by piece, mosaic hearts,
Infinite tales in a gleaming sweep,
Mirrored reflections, secrets keep.

Ceramic Interpretations

Hands of clay, on the wheel they spin,
Crafting life from what's within,
Each form a whisper, a silent plea,
Ceramic tales of what could be.

Shapes emerging, so raw, so true,
In earthen tones and sapphire blue,
Every curve, a testament strong,
In the kiln, where dreams belong.

Glazes capture the fire's light,
Transforming earth in hues so bright,
Each vessel a story, ancient and new,
Crafted carefully through and through.

The potter's touch, so tender and wise,
Sculpting futures before our eyes,
In every pot, a life's refrain,
Miracles shaped from joy and pain.

Forms that whisper, forms that shout,
Tales we ponder and dream about,
Ceramic worlds of heart and mind,
In clay, our spirits find.

Embers in Crayon

In a world of wax and hue,
Flames of red and blue,
Drawing dreams that never end,
With colors that transcend.

Silent whispers, paper bound,
Vivid phantoms all around,
Sparks that flit in silence deep,
Colored ashes that we keep.

Painted stories, ember lights,
Crayon's magic, silent nights,
Softest touches, sparks anew,
In shades of gold and sapphire blue.

Crafted visions, tenderly,
Flicker in their artistry,
Fires of youth and purest grace,
Drawn in each child's embrace.

In this realm of art and flame,
Whispers of the heart proclaim,
Unseen embers, burning bright,
In each crayon's vivid light.

Decorations of the Psyche

Veils of thought, unbound by form,
Decorations of the mind reborn,
Ethereal brushstrokes, visions wild,
Puzzles played by dreamer's child.

Silent tapestries unfold,
Within the heart, stories told,
Mirrors bend, the truth obscure,
In these pages, thoughts endure.

Labyrinths of memory spun,
Twine and thread, every one,
Ornate patterns, whispers near,
Shadows dance, the end unclear.

Ephemeral symphonies weave,
Echoes of what we believe,
Fragments form in abstract phase,
Mind's kaleidoscopic maze.

Decorations, delicate, fine,
Adorn the corridors of mind,
Specters roaming, secrets keep,
In this chamber, thoughts do seep.

Fleeting Mosaics

Fragments of a visage seen,
In the light that barely gleams,
Shards of memory, moments pass,
Through the panes, a shattered glass.

In each piece, a world confined,
Stories woven, hearts entwined,
Colors merge, then softly part,
In this dance, the fleeting art.

Ephemeral, the patterns shift,
Canvas of the soul adrift,
Mosaics fading with the dawn,
Evanescent dreams are drawn.

Time's a brush and breath so brief,
Crafting joy and scripted grief,
Capturing the love and pain,
Fleeting moments in the rain.

Fragments fall, yet beauty stays,
In the midst of life's arrays,
Mosaics build, then slip away,
In this world, we drift and sway.

Silk and Inspiration

Threads of silk, spun by muse,
Inspiration's tender hues,
Flowing through the artist's hand,
Weaving worlds we understand.

Textures whisper, soft and true,
Dreams are dyed in colors new,
In the touch, a story weaves,
Silk and thought, the soul believes.

Gossamer thoughts, fragile skeins,
Wishful threads in artist's veins,
Boundless visions, gently glide,
Silk and spirit, side by side.

Patterns born in silence deep,
Where imagination sleeps,
Touched by grace, the fabrics glow,
Inspiration's gentle flow.

In each thread, a wonder lies,
Woven with the heart's own ties,
Silk and musings intertwine,
Crafting beauty, line by line.

Canvas of Emotions

A stroke of blue, serene and pure,
Whispers softly, emotions free.
A touch of red, a heart's allure,
In passion's grip, eternally.

Golden hues blend sorrow's weight,
In shadows dark, in light's embrace.
Emerald dreams, they roam and wait,
Within the canvas, hidden grace.

In gray and white, reflections clear,
Of moments past, of time's refrain.
Each color tells a tale so dear,
Of joyful bliss, and silent pain.

The palette speaks a language old,
In vibrant tones, emotions shared.
A canvas painted, stories told,
In strokes of life, bade never spare.

Mixes merge and feelings meld,
Creation forms, a soul revealed.
A world within the frame is held,
Canvas of emotions, unconcealed.

Echoes in Color

Through tapestries of vibrant hues,
An echo sounds from heart to heart.
In every shade, a tale accrues,
Where whispered tones of life impart.

Crimson shadows dance and play,
In twilight's soft, embracing glow.
Emerald waves in breezes sway,
Where echoes in the colors flow.

Glistening pools of azure dreams,
Reflect the past, the present now.
In lilac light, which softly gleams,
The echoes leave their silent vow.

A sepia tone, a memory,
Reminds of days that swiftly go.
In echoes of tranquility,
In palettes rich, emotions show.

The canvas brought to life with care,
Holds echoes of what's been and gone.
In colors bright, emotions dare,
To whisper truths, they paint upon.

Masterpiece of the Mind

Within the artist's fervent gaze,
A world of wonder takes its form.
Through crafted lines, and colored maze,
A masterpiece begins to warm.

Dreams take flight on wings of thought,
In vibrant scenes above, below.
With every brushstroke, worlds are wrought,
In endless streams that ebb and flow.

Textures weave a tale untold,
In every corner, secrets hide.
A symphony of visions bold,
Awakens, draws the mind inside.

From abstract swirls to vivid skies,
The masterpiece of mind does spring.
In infinite and boundless ties,
To thoughts and dreams, its heart does cling.

Each color, stroke, and whispered trace,
Reveals the soul, the spirit deep.
In every part, a sacred space,
A mind's creation, secrets keep.

Whispers in Paint

In twilight's hush, the whispers start,
A language spoken, soft and faint.
Each brush a voice, each stroke a heart,
Transporting dreams through whispers in paint.

A moonlit scene, serene and still,
The colors dance in silver streams.
They weave a tale with artful skill,
Of twilight whispers, sunlit dreams.

Through subtle hues, emotions blend,
In shadows deep, in light's embrace.
The painted whispers never end,
Thoughts captured in their silent grace.

A canvas speaks in tones so clear,
Of joy and sorrow, love and fear.
The whispers linger, drawing near,
With every stroke, a heart sincere.

In every line, a story's told,
Of whispered thoughts in colors bold.
Inpainted realms where dreams unfold,
Whispers in paint, a heart's own hold.

Milton Keynes UK
Ingram Content Group UK Ltd.
UKHW021029230724
445880UK00003B/32